BEST
BOARD MEMBER
EVER